Figures in a Landscape

PHOENIX POETS

GAIL MAZUR

Figures in a Landscape

THE UNIVERSITY OF CHICAGO PRESS
Chicago & London

GAIL MAZUR is Distinguished Writer-in-Residence at Emerson College and the founding director of the Blacksmith House Poetry Series in Cambridge, Massachusetts. She is the author of five books of poems, most recently *They Can't Take That Away from Me* (2001), a finalist for the National Book Award; and *Zeppo's First Wife: New and Selected Poems* (2005), a finalist for the Paterson Poetry Prize and the Los Angeles Times Poetry Prize, and winner of the Massachusetts Book Prize.

The University of Chicago Press, Chicago 60637
The University of Chicago Press, Ltd., London
© 2011 by The University of Chicago
All rights reserved. Published 2011
Printed in the United States of America
20 19 18 17 16 15 14 13 12 11   1 2 3 4 5

ISBN-13: 978-0-226-51441-3 (paper)
ISBN-10: 0-226-51441-2 (paper)

Library of Congress Cataloging-in-Publication Data
Mazur, Gail.
    Figures in a landscape / Gail Mazur.
       p. cm. —(Phoenix poets)
    ISBN-13: 978-0-226-51441-3 (pbk. : alk. paper)
    ISBN-10: 0-226-51441-2 (pbk. : alk. paper)
    I. Title. II. Series: Phoenix poets.
    PS3563.A987F54 2011
    811'.54—dc22   2010028026

♾ The paper used in this publication meets the minimum requirements of the American National Standard for Information Sciences—Permanence of Paper for Printed Library Materials, ANSI Z39.48-1992.

for MICHAEL, *in everything*

CONTENTS

ACKNOWLEDGMENTS

Poems in this book have previously appeared, some in slightly different versions, in the following publications:

AGNI: "American Scene, 1935"

Court Green: "Borges in Cambridge, 1967"

Free Verse: "To the Makers," "Dear Migraine"

Literary Imagination: "Poem," "To the Women of My Family,"
    "Another Form," "Concordance to a Life's Work,"

Memorious: "Shipwreck," "Notes in Chalk on a Ruined Bridge,"
    "History of My Timidity," "Inward Conversation"

Ploughshares: "The Island," "Late September"

Provincetown Arts: "While You Were Out," "Poem at the End of
    August"

Salmagundi: "Post-Pastoral," "Wedding Album," "Isaac Rosenberg,"
    "F & the Interpretation of Dreams," "Daisy, Daisy"

Slate: "Hermit," "The Age," "Figures in a Landscape," "In Another
    Country"

Smartish Pace: "Little Tempest"

Tikkun: "October"

"Poem" appeared in *Pushcart Prize XXXIV: Best of the Small Presses*
    (Wainscott, NY: Pushcart Press, 2010).

"Borges in Cambridge, 1967" was published as a limited edition broadside (Boston: Arrowsmith Press, 2007).

"Little Tempest" was installed on the Boston Institute for Contemporary Arts' Harbor Walk (October 2007).

And my deep gratitude to the Radcliffe Institute for Advanced Studies for the warmth and vibrant enthusiasm of its support.

One

HERMIT

In ancient Greece, a man could withdraw into the desert
to praise his gods in solitude—

he'd live out his days by himself in a cave of sand.
Eremos, Greek for desert—you could look it up.

Hermit crabs live mostly alone
in their self-chosen hermitages, they learn young

to muscle their soft asymmetrical bodies
into abandoned mollusk shells.

Without shells, those inadequate bodies
wouldn't have survived the centuries,

so they tuck their abdomens and weak back legs inside
the burden they'll carry on their backs.

It was Aristotle who first observed
they could move from one shell to another.

But sometimes a hermit crab is social—
sometimes a sandworm, a ragworm,

will live with it inside a snail shell.
And sometimes when the crab outgrows its shell

it will remove its odd companion
and bring it along to a new larger shell.

(The Greeks who taught the Western world
what could be achieved by living together

were also the first in that world to work out
a philosophical justification for living alone.)

If the home it chooses isn't vacant
it will use its large pincer claw to extract

the old inhabitant—usually a dead, or dying,
or less aggressive hermit crab.

Then it drags its spiral shell, its adopted history,
sideways, scrabbling across the wet sand.

That's where you see them,
when the tide is out, on the flats.

At high tide, the weight of the shell
is lessened by the upward pressure of water,

so he can forage for plankton, algae,
sea morsels on the ocean floor.

Actually, he neither "chooses," nor "inherits,"
the mollusk's shell, he has no choice

but to live in it, to lug it with him
everywhere until it's his time to move again.

No shell he inhabits will be his home forever.
Restless, driven, Darwinian,

where he lives today might not please
or fit him tomorrow. I could tell you more,

the flats are seething with unlikely creatures
and remnants of life where life's been unfastened.

According to Tarot, the hermit has internalized
life's lesson to the point where he *is* the lesson.

And you, Gail, though you seem almost frozen,
are you sure you won't abandon

the crowded, calcified armor of your story,
of what was given, what freely chosen—

POEM

They said the mind is an ocean,
but sometimes my mind is a pond
circular, shady,

obscure and surrounding the pond,
scrub oak, poison ivy, inedible
low hanging berries,

and twined with the berries, catbrier;
pond where I once swam to a raft
and climbed on, sun drying,

warming my young skin, boys—
that century.
They said the mind or they said something else—

another metaphor: metaphor,
the very liquid glue that helped the worlds—
tangible, solid and, oh, metaphysical—make sense;

and now, fearsome beings in the thick dark water,
but what?—snapping turtles, leeches,
creatures that sting . . .

Who were *they* to say such a thing?
—Or do I have that wrong?
The mind an ocean glorious infinite salty

teeming with syllables,
their tendrils filtered by greeny light?
They don't always get it *right*, do they?

No, it is an unenchanting thing,
the mind: unmusical, small
a dangerous hole, and stagnant,

murk and leaf-muck at the bottom,
mind an idea of idea-making,
idea of place, place to swim home to—

No, to swim away from, to drown, no, to float—

THE AGE

For what seemed an infinite time there were nights
that were too long. We knew a little science, not enough,

some cosmology. We'd heard of dark matter, we'd been assured
although it's everywhere, it doesn't collide, it will never slam

into our planet, it somehow obeys a gentler law of gravity,
its particles move through each other. We'd begun to understand

it shouldn't frighten us that we were the universe's debris,
or that when we look up at the stars, we're really looking back.

It was hard to like what we knew. We wanted to live
in the present, but it was dark. Ignorance

was one of our consolations. The universe was expanding
at an accelerating rate, we'd been told we were not at its center,

that it had no center. And how look forward with hope,
if not by looking up? I told the others we ought to study

history again, history teaches us more than erasures,
more than diminutions, there'd be something for us there.

I also dared to say we could begin to work at things again,
to make things, that I thought the hours of light would lengthen,

that nature still works that way. We would have a future.
Up to then we'd been observing anniversaries only

of mistakes and catastrophes, the darkness seemed to
blanket, to contain our terrible shame. I don't know

if anyone listened to me, it doesn't matter. Gradually,
afternoons began seeping back. As I'd promised, the children

could walk home from school in the freshening light,
they seemed more playful, singing nonsensical songs

so marvelous catbirds wanted to mimic them. Why say anything,
why tell them the endless nights would return? Listen to them,

the name of a new leader they trust on their lips, *O O O* they chant,
and I hear like one struggling to wake from a mournful dream.

THE ISLAND

Was I the last one waiting? Epochs passed,
tides tossed the island twice each day, sometimes

a lazy shushing, sometimes violent—then
tides would frighten me, count-down clocks striking

off the muzzy days and nights. Mosses grew
around me—pin cushion, pale shield, old man's

beard. One gray day, walking on the sand,
I found a wooden shoe last, size 4, stamped

1903, the cobbler who'd worked with it
long gone—yet why only now had it washed

ashore? And one night, I saw six peonies
tossed on the rocks—Sarah Bernhardts, I thought—

fringed yellow hearts, their palest pink petals
tinged vermilion, strewn, shipwrecked children,

lonely drowned bodies white in the moon's glow.
Where does anything come from?

I picked my way over granite to gather them,
then brought them back to the damp old cabin

where their frail heads drooped from a Chinese vase,
nodding feelingly at the dead child's shoe.

Then, a little interlude of pure joy, amnesiac,
so *human*—then hail, rain, wind, the flailing trees.

TO THE MAKERS

You were like famous cities with rivers and traffic,
with architecture from ingenious eras,

with protest marches and festivals, museums and pharmacies
and criminal pleasures—

all the essentials needed to endure. Reading you,
I re-visit your structures of grids and avenues, your alleys,

I follow overgrown paths,
I re-visit the terror and joy of being lost,

the ways to court discomfort, to dare chaos,
the knowledge of drowning in a pitch-dark harbor.

Tyranny and wars advanced in your histories,
also infirmities of soul and body

were your portion, yet you were not yearning only,
not heartbreak only,

you were not the loneliest people alive.
There was your work, and then, you had one another,

you spoke with gods and heroes,
you cherished your conversations in many languages.

It is true, you were secretive, observers—spies—
but that was as it has to be,

it was only your work you were given to serve.
You weren't mere investigators of useless things,

the pragmatic seemed no more or less
suggestive to you than articles of turbulence

or rapture—strands of hair in a basin,
light in a dusty stairwell

a pitcher of sangria, woe and laughter,
the feel in the hand of a broken thing.

Day by day, your lives were a tumult of beginnings.
When you began, you couldn't know—

this you keep showing me—
where your constructions would lead,

what you made you made from the inchoate,
muscled and shaped not toward the monumental

but toward a form of truth that would matter,
the inaccessible become necessary.

Though I am speaking to you, I'm not alone

nurtured by your art,
even today you animate the minutiae

of the vast, unsigned cosmos,
and though the twentieth century ended without you,

now, decades after your precipitate departures,
your pages are still touched by many,

still touch many,
and the lit screens you never used sing your lines.

SHIPWRECK
—Winter, Wellfleet, 2008

Sweet carcass of an ark, the past's oaken belly—
what the sands had buried a storm uncovered
high on Newcomb Hollow beach; a hull,

round wooden pegs, tool marks that tell
its serious age, ribs like the bony cage
of a Great White whale, washed up

on the shoals a decade after the Civil War, a schooner,
archaeologists say, converted to a barge—
they think she carried coal up the Atlantic coast

from an impoverished post-War South,
coal that washed ashore on the outer Cape
to the hardscrabble townspeople's shivering relief.

In a few weeks, they're sure the tides will resettle her,
she'll be washed back out to sea or she'll merge again,
fill with the coarse sands shifting beneath your feet.

Homely, heavy, sea-scoured, why should she seem
a venerable thing, spiritual, why should you long
to touch her, to stretch out under the March sun

in the long smooth silvery frame of a cradle
or curl like an orphaned animal on the hand-cut planks
and caress the marks, the trunnels, with your mittened paws?

Is it that she hints much yet tells little of the souls lost
with her, the mystery of survival, the depths she's traveled?
Has she heard the music on the ocean floor, instrumentation

of Mantis Shrimp, the *bong bong* of Humming Fish?
Why does the day, all blues and greys, feel transcendental?
She's a remnant, a being almost completely effaced, yet to you

still resonant—can anything this gone be consecrated? Experts
have examined the braille of her hull, weighed the evidence
and they declare, *It's another secret the ocean burped up*,

nothing but a blip, a brief reappearance, once rowdy,
rough with purpose, now not even a container, holding
nothing, revealing nothing. . . . But aren't you also a singular secret

Nature burped up, hurled flailing into the air from the start,
hungry for light, holding onto whatever buoys you,
alive, kicking, even when you know you're going down?

WHILE YOU WERE OUT

The schooner *Hindu* dropped its sails, the bay was calm.
An unflappable egret posed alone on your studio rail.

The telephone rang. If this were a pink slip torn
from a memo pad, I couldn't say who'd called, or when

or why we'd fought so bitterly last night. Two small boys
called out, high chords of hilarity, tossing dead horseshoe crabs

as far as they could, not far at all. Mailer traipsed along the flats
in his yellow bikini, his gray curls wild, pugnacious masculine

overhang of belly, his arthritic little bulldog panting to keep up,
a slender girl beside him jotting nattered oddments of his prose.

For a minute, our era's brute injustices felt almost settled,
its perpetual wars the memoir of a battle-scarred contrarian

enlightening his disciple. I wanted to be sun-drunk, asleep to everything.
Where had you gone? A slow August day and you were out,

and this is my memo to you. I walked on the wet sand
as the incoming tide insinuated contradictions,

I collected beach glass, not questioning the pleasure
I took combing for sand-washed fragments metamorphosed

from bottles sailors tossed long ago into a suffering sea.
Purposeless day, reading random pages of old books—astronomy,

elegies, a Venetian mystery, greedy for good information. Greedy,
I went to the garden and clipped pink blooms from my Butterfly Bush

and deep crimson blooms from the Love Lies Bleeding. The perfume
of our one life permeated the rooms, contrition's delicate bouquet.

All along the shore, in wooden houses vulnerable as ours
to fire and wind and time, others may have been fuming

or weeping, too, their human despairs let loose on one another,
little microcosmic wars, everyone standing in the breach.

Tonight, Mars will be nearer the moon than it's been in 60,000 years,
and though the radio claims it's bright red to the naked eye,

all week we've raked the night skies and only seen something flashier
and slightly pinker than all the blushing stars we can't identify:

timeless celestial chart, imperishable astral chart that terrifies.
Why quarrel now? Why tap deadly cracks in our little eggshell house?

LATE SEPTEMBER

Now, from the sweet fragrance of roses,
bitterness stings our nostrils. The bay's
withdrawn from us, the beach is littered
with broken things—splintered oars, bits
of old clay pipe from a long ago shipwreck,
fragments of china plates. Enchanting, those days
my townspeople scavenged rare cargo,
furnishing their long winters with random wares.

Now, the wind from two directions turns
soft dubious summer to a hard estate. Now,
when we know death is near, we walk
with more courage, but slowly, alongside
cavorting dogs. And soon he and I will wade
together into the cold homecoming wave.

after Sereni

OCTOBER

Days of Awe.
Month of our parents' deaths.

Reddening dogwood and sugar maple,
deep dark dramatic red of sumac
along a Cape road, and in the city,
jackets donned, then at mid-day, shed.

Nature's refrain, the return of losses,
piercing glory of the leaves' palette
before the tossing windy rains,
slop and decay, the burial under snow.

And yet, a new year, new breath:

repetition of stories that once wounded
or bewildered and now delight—
actual stories, after all
this time: Funny. Sad. Slight.

Memories, misquotes.
Days of reflection, of reconciliation.

Their faults now only foibles
and all the meannesses and pathos,
hoarding and generosities,
the stoniness and warmth,

part of their allure,
part of the layered shapeliness.
Enduring, granitic characters
at last achieved.

With acceptance of them,
some also perhaps of yourself.
It is not your job to finish the task,
but neither are you free to abandon it.

NOTES IN CHALK ON A RUINED BRIDGE

When I first read the phrase man's inhumanity
to man in the other world I found it elegant
but inadequate though I was moved by it

In the beginning the five of us were angry
then frightened—those sooty days still
days of hope and imagination

Hope and imagination
each one necessary to the other
that is what I thought

Then we had a sheepish sense someone would come
to feed us to organize our group
to herd us to a city with parks and fountains

For a time I would repeat my favorite words
and my mother's choice unprintable ones
and my uncle's forbidden ones

my children's exuberant babble of wonder
none of the others shared my interest
but I would recite alphabetically for instance

my favorite adjectives all the birds
I could name authors from seven continents
for Antarctica I invented the author Per Mission

just to live in my mind in the gone world

Still most mornings
or what I estimated inside our noxious cloud
was morning

we'd wait together we were very hungry
small starving animals voles and mice with round ears
feared us as we feared them

because we'd lost confidence in ourselves
and shared no vocabulary to discuss
what we'd been severed from or where we were

I lost one then two then more Latinate
or Indian-rooted words I remember liking
and slowly the names of invisible constellations

If there'd been wind they'd have been words
in the wind after some time the acidic air
ate them all then I spoke no more

because there was no one left no one to listen
no one but me to care and I don't know if I care
every stone here at the bridge is coated

with the salt of my people's unshed tears
what is caring anyway but clinging to hope
which also clung to me so under the broken stones

I could find this package of white chalk
each cylinder perfect whole and my dream
became not that we'd talk again

but that you would arrive and you would know
how to read my dead mongrel language
and you would read it my message before

the great rain erased it
before the trestle disintegrated
after I was no longer hungry or waiting—

FIGURES IN A LANDSCAPE

We were two figures in a landscape,
in the middle distance, in summer.

In the foreground, twisty olive trees,
a mild wind made the little dry leaves tremble.

Then, of course, the horizon,
the radiant blue sky.

(The maker was hungry for light,
light silvered the leaves, a stream.)

I liked to think, for your sake,
the scene was Italian, 17th century. . . .

Viewed from here, we resembled one another
though in truth we were unalike—

and we were tiny, he'd kept us small
so the painting would be landscape, not anecdote.

We were *made* things, deftly assembled
but beginning to show wear—

you, muscular, sculptural,
and I was I, we were different, we had a story.

On good days we found comedy in that,
pratfalls and also great sadness.

Sun moved across the sky and lowered
until you, then I, were in shadow, bereft.

The Renaissance had ended—
we'd long known we were mortal.

In shadow, I held the wild daisies and cosmos
we'd been gathering for the table.

Then the sky behind us pinked and enflamed
the landscape where we were left

to our own reinvention, two silhouettes
who still had places they meant to travel,

who were not abstractions—had you pricked them
they'd have bled, alizarin crimson.

I wanted to walk by myself awhile
but I'd always been afraid to lose you

and the naked olive groves were hovering
as if to surround you.

That was the problem:
I craved loneliness; I needed the warmth of love.

If no one looks at us, do we or don't we disappear?
The landscape would survive without us.

When you're in it, it's not landscape
any more than the horizon's a line you can stand on.

March 2009

Two

HISTORY OF MY TIMIDITY

Little sister, little fiddlehead, you unfurled early in me,
your leaflets and blades swirled in my cerebellum,
though I would stand in the yard, muttering

Do not forget the plum blooming in the thicket!

When I'd slouch out on the longest legs in town
I knew it was true
what our Lithuanian grandmother said:

there were no other giantesses here like me,
though she watched for Cossacks
from her jalousied window, afraid for us all.

I wore our brother's shirts, mother's skirts,
outsized shoes, my darling Clementine sandals—
"herring boxes without topses." Dear homuncula,

if I was fated to be large, I wanted not to live
in the shadow of something small,
but to be the flamingo flaring on the lawn, tropical,

not the hermit turtle aestivating in pond mud—

What I wanted: flamingoes, and the world
in my little radio under the pillow,
all the lights out, you asleep, my soft-boned other.

31

I wanted music, jazz, comedy, Allen's Alley,
Digger O'Dell the fr-r-riendly undertaker!
Intoxicating jokes in the nights!

And blues in the swooning nights, and Frankie Laine
crooning to you and me, *No tears, no sighs,*
we both have a lifetime before us and parting is not good-bye,

We'll be together again. O Timidity,
we *were* together, you, my piddling self,
fermenting resentment, you, pissing on my desires—

like those murderous shy people of the bayous,
crouching with their muskets behind the cypress knees.
—Even now, the memory of you shames me,

drags me back to our twinned days, swamps me
in its black waters. Sister I abandoned, little one,
in the day-world I pretended to be you, flaunting nothing

in the no-privacy of our body—but in my internal exile,
something else, a body steered by the rocky story
of its time, wanting the hula hoop, the hullabaloo,

wanting the flimflam of flirtation, then wanting *more,*
high-stepping through the muck away from you,
night after night, to get *more,* leaving you,

you—square-eyed, despairing, watching me go.

DEAR MIGRAINE,

You're the shadow shadow lurking in me
and the lunatic light waiting in that shadow.

Ghostwriter of my half-life, intention's ambush
I can't prepare for, ruthless whammy

you have me ogling a blinding sun,
my right eye naked even with both lids closed—

glowering sun, unerring navigator
around this darkened room, you're my laser probe,

I'm your unwilling wavelength,
I can never transcend your modus operandi,

I've given up trying to outsmart you,   '
and the new thinking says I didn't invent you—

whatever you were to me I've outgrown,
I don't need you, but you're tenacity embodied,

tightening my skull, my temple, like plastic wrap.
Many times, I've traveled to a dry climate

that wouldn't pander to you, as if the great map
of America's deserts held the key to a pain-free future,

but you were an encroaching line in the sand,
then you were the sand. We've spent the best years

of my life intertwined: wherever I land
you entrap me in the unraveled faces

of panhandlers, their features my features—
you, little death I won't stop for, little death

luring me across your footbridge to the other side,
oblivion's anodyne. Soon—I can't know where or when—

we'll dance ache to ache again on my life's fragments,
one part abandoned, the other abundance—

ASYMMETRICAL MILLAY NOVEMBER

The parents, all dressed up, leave for the funeral
of Edna Millay in Provincetown,

saying, *You stay here in Auburndale and wash
the dining room rug*

(a gray rectangle with a row of circles at one edge,
asymmetrical,

and a burnt-orange stain of squash-cinder soup
shaped like the state of Maine).

When I said I'd like to go with them,
I knew *everything* about Millay—

I didn't refer to her as "Vincent,"
a tactical disguise of my erudition—

Father said *No*, he didn't want to feel *belittled*,
that was how he'd feel, with me there.

Confusing—could I make my tall, gallant father feel small,
who glowed with pride in me?

Then Mother, she was so complicated, smiled, *Child,
I'd have loved to have had you there*—

so what *tense* was that? Latin School, Radcliffe,
Portia Law. Again,

I felt the fool with her, large and childish—
and angry.

I already held the galvanized bucket of suds,
our hoard of rags, a brushy tool.

—Why be so desperate to pay respects to Millay,
my embarrassing old enthusiasm?

Actually, the stain was the shape of Cape Cod,
its crooked arm, and Provincetown

the clenched fist, where, I thought, wrongly, Millay
was born, not Camden, Maine,

and actually, that arm and fist were cranberries
from the Truro bog,

like torn bleeding rubies on the gray carpet.
Not a bad metaphor,

or so I thought. I wasn't yet the poet
I wished to be.

I also thought we should phone the Company
that comes to people's houses

with machines that swish and scour dirty carpets.
My clueless extravagance.

Why should Mother go instead in her silk blouse
with the bow at the throat?

Everyone she knew on the Cape was gone:
the butcher, the baker, the candlestick maker

she told me were all old Reds; and her friends,
the hermit and Farmer Chiles,

and also some vile sons-of-bitches—
just a lot of fallen rotting logs.

Please, I knew her, I know all about her,
I persisted, *the affairs, the candle burning*

at both ends, the going back and forth all night
on the ferry, the drunkenness,

the endless sonnets, the fatal tumble down her stairs
in Austerlitz.

But Mother just glowered and hissed: "That awful
tacky book—I read it."

And that was that.

Outwitted, outmaneuvered. I should have been ready,
I knew how she thought.

I stayed home, scrubbing and teary, a teetotaler
drunk on self-pity

until I switched on the light in my dream-misted room
and lay listening

to waves crashing against the wooden pilings,
their pure persistence

part of the primordial cycle, its blur of gifts
and retractions,

its visitations and departures. I was shaken
and stirred then

by the dream-mind's odd willful concoctions,
so I thought

of the poems I loved that weren't dead at all
though my parents still were.

TO THE WOMEN OF MY FAMILY

Fierce, frightened, fragmented,
my women,

for the flower of hope for years
I meant

to apologize, that it bloomed in me
without nourishment—

or nourishment was the silvered mirage
in the mirror

greeting me one morning when I was young—
fascinating,

and foreign: hope. Whose sunstruck face
was that

but my own? Why did only the men
make music

in our family? One sang, off-key
but all the time,

the other played piano, the clarinet,
the flute,

then the many beautiful instruments
of consolation—

songs, like optimism, that couldn't really
be shared.

What I wanted, what I wanted to want then,
was for hope

to be divisible, multiplicable,
like the lilies

and the irises, and I'd have divided
the corms,

delivered some to you and then planted
them there

to wave for a week in the breezes
each spring.

The tall blue iris in my Victorian yard—
I'd keep

that plant for myself *and* let it blossom
for you,

its gorgeous unfurled petals, a flower
that exposes

itself, then is rained on, breaks,
dies, and yet

returns, tough and unkillable.
My apology,

my desire for you to have this, too,
somehow

was ungrateful, insulting to you,
my mothers.

I was presumptuous to claim I could
fathom

your wounds born when you were born,
hostages,

as I thought, to your century's contusions.
Of course,

you would interpret powerful injuries
in the blind

careless glances of women and men, strangers
barreling by,

abstracted, benign or malignant but
seigneurial

in their conspicuous indifference.
You knew

the foot was in the aisle to trip us,
not accidental.

Who feared more, you, or I?

We weren't, were we, Darwin's worms,
working and digesting,

useful to the earth and its cultivars,

our own deaths always the only goal?
If I thought

that was the way you lived, pain
always arriving

where you'd prepared the soil, the soul,
for it,

I apologize, I was wrong the way a child
is wrong

for half my life, blind not to see in your
forward moves

courage, the great distances you negotiated,
all of you,

not to see the ground you covered. Wrong
not to know

without hope there would be no courage,
without courage,

no purpose. I was mistaken but lucky,
though it took,

I am sorry, half my life to admit
my excitations,

my wishes, my expectations. Lucky
to feel

my own blessed wanting so much,
even now,

here it is—*so wanton, so extravagant!*—
and here I am

in this minute, almost free to express it.

ANOTHER FORM

for Elizabeth King

Another form of penance, brooding
in my blue garage, renouncing meaning,

renouncing marvel, my door closed
on the hot exuberant garden, its pale

larkspur and its deep blue larkspur
giddy in the sea breeze, no memory of

the dry seeds I'd scattered randomly
last September, my blue shades pulled down

now against the mesmerizing bay.
Another form of selfishness if I could have

clapped my hands to my ears—but
I listened: *Everything's turning yellow,*

my skin, my nails, my teeth, my eyes.
On the phone that morning, I couldn't look

at green water or blue flowers. Who teaches
anyone to drift secretly from conversation,

to keep conversant with the teasing self?
Was it too late to enroll in that school?

Would that have been another form
of indenture? I stayed in one position

until noon, another form of mourning,
my notebook closed on my thigh, my hand's

grip on the pen noncommittal.
Lost in the echoes of sadness

and ruination—*unmaking*,
yet another form of penance—and then

dear friend, this quotation floated toward me
from faraway: *If you want to know who I am,*

try to make what I make. And then I thought,
Someday this sorrow may take another form.

IN ANOTHER COUNTRY

For months I perched on the surface of her life.

I sat at her oak desk trying to write,
ate at her table, holding her fork in my right hand,

turned the pages of one of the books,
then another, from her alphabetized shelves:

Mandelstam. Merwin. Miłosz.
O'Hara. Petrarch. Pound.

Outside, no river, but there was a ship canal,
ships delivering or carrying oil away.

The city smelled of oil natives didn't smell,
the grass was coarse and spongy.

There were many things I liked: her Saarinen chair,
the fanfare of school buses arriving across the street,

the warm humid air, Spanish moss festooning
the live oaks everywhere, the white fossil granite

her department's building was made of—
exquisite whorls, the chambered nautilus scattered

over its 3 stories, precise tiny impressions
of ancient sea creatures I couldn't identify. . . .

I dressed in the dark, pulling my shoes out
from under her double bed, blind to their color,

I went to her job, wearing one blue shoe, one maroon
(maroon for Houston, blue for distant Boston?)

—my students thought it was the style somewhere,
it made them shy, they'd study my feet admiringly.

Sometimes before sleep, I'd sit in the womb chair
her mother-in-law had left her, the color of beet soup;

sometimes I'd lie in bed with her insomnia, listening
to the downstairs neighbor cough his irradiated lungs away,

my bed a space capsule, my head floating,
me thinking, *Houston, we've got a problem!*

—But those shoes, the maroon and the blue:
as the joke goes, I had another pair just like it at home.

POST-PASTORAL

Look, I said to myself, go sit in the woods
until something happens. Your childhood forest,
that old Eden, could be a library you've taken

for granted and forsaken. The outdoors, to me,
had always been backcloth, a given, but that day
I determined to be a novice, to read

the remaindered world as if it were the World Book.
Go rusticate, I said, the brown itch of dead
leaves is nothing to sneeze at, nor the ingenious

design of acorn caps, nor the rough bark
of scrub pine at your back. So I walked in
and made my appointment to be a student

of those trees, of the red ant nesting in mulch
and debris, and the pale waxy Indian pipe,
a phantom the Wampanoag call "ghost plant."

My whole life I'd loved one twisted beech tree,
my gray climbing tree, now it was leafless,
dry, and tired, and I came up to its shoulder.

Because I'd viewed nature without curiosity
the Latin names in my new field guide
genus and species, and the common names,

the stems and stones and roots, enhanced for me
the living birds and insects themselves,
the invisible rustlings, the mosses' secrecies,

at home as I'd always been in the lives of pages.
But when I began to look, what could come to me
came to me: I saw toads the size of my thumbnail,

so cute I didn't need to know their names
or name them beyond *toad*; I spotted the dung
of a red fox; a white-tailed deer grazing

on foliage in the cedar swamp. I didn't assume,
as I always had, to be loaded with information
was as good as being loaded with wisdom.

One day, I stood in the dappling greens,
trembling with the emancipated joy
a clever child might take in *spelling*, in getting

every word right, the way the world opens to her,
the world feels possible to master. Could that be
how my grandmother felt a hundred years ago

in Maine, a poor immigrant, at seventeen
only ten years distant from the pogroms
of the Old Country, studying alone

each night the math she'd teach to ruffians
and the nice farm kids the next cold morning
in a one-room schoolhouse in the new land—

each day a triumph for her, *learning* a kind
of moral victory over her own foreignness,
her ignorance. But here I was, an urban woman

in mid-life sitting on the hard ground of the mortal
American landscape, vibrating in the tactile
and the Latin and the grand canopy

of Mashpee trees, telling herself, Look, look, look,
and looking. *The question is not what you look at,*
but what you see, Thoreau said, so I went

barefoot down the warm soft pine needle path
to the lake to swim above herring minnows
and stripey pickerel, I saw mint for my tea

and tiny blueberries with powdery skins.
I stayed until late, fireflies, *Lampyridae*,
lit the black nights, and bats—fluttering,

coasting and diving darkly above the tree line—
my old bugaboos cast malign silhouettes,
sinister cartoons on the waning moon.

Those summers, I lived in the beech forest,
fagus sylvatica, the final forest.
A brief chapter, really, naming the mushrooms

and mayflowers, defying jet trails from the air base,
mourning the ugly dying catfish, uttering
syllables that had been uttered for eons

before me in nature's homely vernaculars,
savoring a truly ancient language, alive
with what had once seemed secret knowledge

and would surely seem so to me again,
and then, only then, when I'd begun to feel
at home, when I knew I would never live

long enough to exhaust it, nor could I
protect it, nor could it protect me,
when I knew I couldn't always return,

couldn't always look and see the thousand
browns, the richness of greens, when I knew grief
was part of me and I would bear it, then I took my leave.

AUTOBIOGRAPHIA MISERERIA

—I was a washashore in murky waters
fishing for a species that hadn't been fished
out yet, I had no radar, no sonar, no
savvy paraphernalia the old pros
carry for the last spawning grounds,

the unruined habitats of blues, or stripers.
I was an unattuned student struggling
like hell to get the gist of an essay on
the thicket of shame and fame she inhabits
(no word or signifier I read rang a bell),

turning charts of stars this way and that
to find some direction, but *niente, nada*—
I was an elderly seamstress in Novgorod,
looking for needles in the burning haystacks
of a stranger's farm, I knew I'd have to pack

and run soon, I was an Alaskan hunter
shooting caribou from a government 'copter
like fish in a barrel, not asking why I did
good animals harm, when a saurian raptor
clipped my propeller. Devolution nightmare,

black night at noon, blinding, no one
to guide me toward what I knew was missing,
some piece I'd dropped along the way, a crucial
fact I'd forgotten. I was the negligent curator
of something rare, I couldn't find my department,

I knew it was on the seventeenth floor,
that I was a lepidopterist, that I was
Nabokov and I'd misplaced my specimens,
butterflies whose wings I'd pinned expertly
to archival paper with just a *soupçon*

of acid, Blues that would have carried on
my name I'd lost in my mid-day breakdown.
Upstairs, in the lab, microscopes, beakers,
pins and needles, my stainless tables,
the crystalline world where silence reigned,

but I was all attrition, no new revisions
of classifications, no metaphysical
speculations affirming the theory
of evolution. Like St. Petersburg
vanishing with the Revolution, and dressed

in polar thermals, I left that world with only my nets
and little labels, I was moving downward
into the deep blue brumal vapors,
cold, defoliated, and truly unknowing,
though I guessed rightly it would be my last expedition.

INWARD CONVERSATION

I'm beginning to understand myself:
I exist in the space my cells leave behind
every seven years when they make room
for a new set of pixels to move in.
Myself: a fleeting entity, made of fugitive parts.
In the first cycles, the transitions refreshed me.
Now, not so much; now,
I make the most of my territory
while those mites rush past me, their time up,
and the next crew of aliens debates moving in.
I'm tough, that's what I know. No matter what
molecular stuff's staggering through the door,
it'll leave me alone soon enough,
so I kick my slippers to the floor,
turn off the light and ignore what's coming.
I relax—I'm introducing my mind
to my mind again. In an incognito world,
it's not myself I won't know.

Three

WEDDING ALBUM

Everyone's here in the pictures, nobody appears
what you'd call pleased—my stunned father looks sweet,
your mother, gowned in scarlet lace décolletage,
loathes us all and won't stop smiling. I seem bride-ish,
blank, I've rehearsed the whole thing. No one's going
to shout *Stop!* when the rabbi in the name
of the Commonwealth invites the congregation
to object to our union. It turns out this is *it*,
we're both quaking, our hands vibrating, both thinking,
This is a terrible mistake, thinking, *I bet we'll pay
for this later*. We don't yet know we're extremely young—
we've been misled by our bodies—but why does no one
else try to protest? You have thrilling 5 o'clock shadow,
a hint of Johnny Stompanato; Gittelsohn's,
the first rabbi to serve in the Marines, chaplain
to all faiths (his Iwo Jima eulogy for his battalion's
dead still famous for its eloquence, the Temple
president claims *almost* like the Gettysburg Address.
Last week, we were counseled in his Temple
Israel office—when he asked if you'd prepared
by reading any books on marriage and you offered
Yes, Madame Bovary, he didn't blink, but holy
moley what could he have been thinking?)
So, we'll get married and de-camp alone, drive off
in your father's old black Chrysler New Yorker
with the white-wall tires. When we stop on the pike

at Howard Johnson's, your mother will be there waving,
saving you a seat beside her—so where are
the Vaseline-lensed cameras? Only four days until
my mid-year exams, needless to say I haven't studied—
for that, I'll also pay later. Soon there'll be babies,
jobs, a succession of small cities. The country's at peace.
We haven't begun our fiery letters to the *Times*.
I think, *We've already done the hard part.*

But now we are here, met on the battlefield
of the future with fly-by-night friends, our nettled
families, the bridesmaids' hysterical seizures—
we're about to make a fine mess of things;
if we're lucky, it won't much matter—do we know
it's all in front of us, we're in the vestibule of it,
the mystery of art, of love, we can almost touch it.

BORGES IN CAMBRIDGE, 1967

Bookish, my bookish friend called you, *bookishness*
the failing grade he gave your genius and his own

after your first Mem Hall lecture on "The Riddle
of Poetry." In that afternoon's amber light,

you spoke without notes, your translucent, blind face
tilted toward the high windows; you seemed to be

gazing heavenward, speaking softly enough to be heard
in Victorian Harvard's memorial to privilege

and its Civil War dead, that first heroic generation
of losses that set Brahmin Boston on its down path.

Outside the old "brick pile," students and bikers
protested the war they hated, war we all hated,

their exhilarating noise filtering, unintelligible
through the indestructible walls, righteous and romantic—

like your romance with Argentina's gauchos,
swashbuckling across the pampas, who'd thrilled your youth;

you'd dreamt of wounding nobly with a sword,
then endured life as a Buenos Aires librarian

in love with books you'd memorized but could no longer
read. How otherworldly, how disarming, you seemed,

telling us Cervantes' La Mancha was meant to be
an ordinary place, not princely—as if he'd written,

you said, "Don Quixote of Kansas City"—Kansas City
and Mass Ave, your two favorite American phrases.

I listened as if the SDS weren't racketing the perimeter
of the Yard, blazing quixotically for a future

like the present with its lovely options but without
the dying, the brutal mutilations. Was I really in the hall

then, or tramping outside—the retrospective Gail
remembers both—I know I marched, my fist raised

defiantly like the other demonstrators, chanting
our chants, month after month—*real* to be mattering,

to spill into the streets, to "be counted," to count for
something: absurdly beautiful, the single-minded ecstasy

of a just cause. Now, memory conflates occasions,
it pauses to hold open my two worlds, offers again

the desperate optimistic din, the quiet lifelike love of art.
The war we thought we'd helped to finish never ends.

AMERICAN SCENE, 1935

My friend the French easel and I, what ecstatic hours
we spent together away from the roasty odors of home,
from gossip and slip-covered chairs,
my dutiful aunts sweating over the Glenwood stove,

my boastful uncles upholstered in their cadmium yellow suits
and nudie-girl ties, the way they pinched my cheeks to kiss me
on the lips. I drew them, not from spite, but they were forms
on the davenport under the dim lamps—lines and shadows.

I used brown paper bags cut into squares, a stick of charcoal.
In charcoal, they weren't tiresome, they looked
interesting. Not just large sausages stuffed into clothing.
I hated those Sundays until I learned to escape:

I married a man who charred the potatoes, blackened the peas,
and let me be. I loved my tools, my palette knife, my canvases,
my tubes of oils. My husband had pretensions to art.
Well, I could have done without him, too.

Now they call my paintings "lonely"— what do they know?
Painting was the only way I knew to scratch where it itched.
The drag of a brush in my hand, getting a roofline right,
marking the cold shadow cast by an open summer door.

Maybe I am slightly inhuman, but I liked old buildings,
water towers, all-night diners, a girl in an orange blouse
finishing her chores. With my easel folded on my back,
everything I've ever needed neatly stored inside it,

I could go anywhere, from the City to the unvarnished main street
of any American town. I'd say *not* lonely: a painting would talk
to me, talk back to me, often it would insist I put down my brush,
would argue that it was finished. I relished those arguments.

Sometimes the painting was right. Sometimes I was. Wasn't that enough?
All I ever wanted to do was to paint sunlight on the side of a house.

ISAAC ROSENBERG

A short man, maybe five-foot-four, born in Maine,
given to depression; a pessimist;
he wanted to be a doctor, I think,
but in the nineteenth century, Jewish,
he applied to dental college instead;
stuck with his name, his height, his discomfort
in his own skin. He had a dead mother;
a stepmother wicked enough to explain
his gloom; two sisters, and two half-brothers
who escaped to New York to become lawyers,
bachelors. You never saw Doc reading
a book—he wasn't the British poet,
shot down at twenty-eight in the Great War
by a German sniper, who wrote the Best Poem
of that war, "Break of Day in the Trenches,"
admired by anti-Semitic Ezra Pound
and T. S. Eliot. Ornery, morose,
but American, so without the specific
tribal dread that news—any article
in the paper—might be bad for the Jews,
fear that tormented his wife and others
plagued by their nightmare memories of flight.
A Republican, only historians knows why,
a pinochle playing state-of-Mainer,
crony of firemen and cops, most cheerful
where his wife Jenny never visited:

the back room of a station house, a night
of cards, cigar smoke, good-natured gags
and jabs, and then years later, in Boston,
in Scollay Square, bright cafeterias
where men met for pie and hot coffee
and commiseration. Loveless marriage
to the tall beauty Jenny; two daughters,
in the 'thirties the Gorgeous Rosenberg
Girls of Brookline; a "genius" son at Harvard,
a lifelong Communist Joe McCarthy
caught up with (then even Doc came to dread
the fifteen-minute television news.)
—Not related to the martyred Ethel
and Julius Rosenberg Rosenbergs either
but could have been. Could he have entered
medical school, could he have beaten
the quota? Who told him no?
A little Jewish tough from north of no-
where, would he have wanted to try?
Was that the if-only of his story?
He wore a Spanish-American War button
he'd found in the Boston Common one autumn.
How could he have written a battle poem?
A bantam cock, once kind of a scrapper,
a bully to Mrs. R, his wife, he loved
his tempestuous daughter, my mother,
and his first grandson, my brother. The year
he died—he'd say "kicked the bucket"—
he taught Jonny some Yiddish I'd never heard
him speak a word of, and that way
helped him pass his graduate German exam.

F & THE INTERPRETATION OF DREAMS

Last night, I dreamt F moved to Becket, Mass.,

to a hickory cabin where every morning,
even in snow, he carries empty Poland
Spring bottles out to his yard, to a pump

two rusty centuries old, or more,
then with one mittened hand on its handle—
rusticating (though he's said he *loathes* nature)—

he fills the 8-ounce plastic bottles,
then shovels a path to the old red barn—
a lumpy half-ruined barn—and milks the cow

and leans the shovel against the lean-to
and carries in the bubbling pail of milk,
the mineral-laden water.... Sometimes I wonder

why I spend the nights dreaming dreams I forget
even as I dream them, why I wake thinking
I haven't dreamt at all, each night a blank

unpopulated space—or I snap to,
knowing a beloved hand or face has wakened me,
and have to switch the light and read

whatever book is lying on the floor.
—Then why should I remember *this* dream,
why *Becket*? Of all places, what brought F here?

Does that mean he, or I, have on our minds
not pastoral retreat, but, maybe, Thomas à Becket,
Eliot's martyred saint, the lean-to his midnight cathedral,

the shovel, nature *itself*, his hair shirt; or,
Samuel Beckett—comical, tough, yet inconsolable
in the landscape of an incoherent world?

Is that me, or F, or neither? Oh, and Poland Spring—
what's that about? Our Old Country,
Kovno gubernia? No, it's *my* Old Country—

Poland—not F's! Sometimes I wonder
if the Past isn't really what *the Old Country* means,
the idealized Past, in every language an epithet

of longing: *the Old Country*, left behind
with youth, with innocence. Idealized
and bitter, yet appetizing, yet bitter

to have lost it, to long to return, to know
it's not there anymore. Or there is a bit
of soil, a pebble, some broken granite slabs

with eroded calligraphic names and dates,
now sidewalk stepping-stones, the only traces
of our families' histories, both F's and mine—

66

the bloody farms, the horses that left the barn,
the pitted nights—Was I so wrong to place him
in that Becket-world we're both unsuited for,

to leave him alone under constellated skies
with a rotting barn, a lean-to,
bubbling milk, the rusty pump, a mitten?

LITTLE TEMPEST

Does it make you more philosophical to sit there
watching the tide come in and finally go back out?

And in between, when you swim in the fluggy bay,
Are you gone from me, floating in astral space?

From our room, I watch you gazing inward
while I turn the pages of The Catastrophe Daily.

It might calm me if you'd come into the house
a minute—you, in the splintery Adirondack chair.

And when the hurricane that's been predicted comes?
Please remember, the last one blew the motel roof

into our neighbor's house, a whole lived-in story
with bedrooms and hall lights gone in a minute;

a young woman stood on the moor, letting swirling sands
lacerate her hands and face—the next morning

did she feel safe, indestructible, strolling raw-faced
around the broken dresser drawers, the backless rocker,

the turquoise toilet seat? Did she know a man had just died
on that sidewalk, while she was out defying the gods?

People were strolling, everyone seemed *pleased*
in the aftermath. That cold clear light. Please come in,

lie to me, tell me our danger's over, a short story,
a passing disaster. *I'm* not philosophical, my mind sticks

in its minute, replaying its feverish fears—little tempest,
where can it go, what can it think it hasn't thought before?

10,000 DAYS

My student has flown off to Utah
to celebrate his first great milestone:

10,000 days living on this earth

Sounds like a lot, even to me

Waiting for me in a bookstore, my friend John read
it takes 10,000 hours to be proficient—

well, a virtuoso—at anything
like a musical instrument, or physics

He wonders if he still has 10,000 hours
to learn to spin on his head

I say, *Too late for that, John!*

Once, my brother the microbiologist
(tens of thousands of lab hours)

was caught
in a flash flood in Little Wild Horse Canyon

There were warning signs but that's how much
he and his wife love those Utah canyons

They'd probably been together 15,000 days
and wanted more, but they could have died then

horribly in a place they both loved
though I think not with equal abandon

I don't tell the 10,000-day-old man
how long it takes before you make the first poem

you keep liking and keep revising
he might not believe it, or it would be irrelevant

but I'd say it took me about 10,000 days on earth
not doing much but living and reading

trying not to count the days of my children's lives
from 1 to 6,000 then

or yours and mine together—
almost 20,000, I'd estimate

if I counted—but I don't count,
don't want to mark our notch on the continuum

when Ron brings me his Utah poem
the one where he's smiling there inside the Delicate Arch

71

CONCORDANCE TO A LIFE'S WORK

Again, air.
Always another answer: *Away!*

Bed, bedroom, bird—black, blue.
Body, book, brain.

Daughter, day, day, day.
Dead—door, down, dream,

eyes face Father:

final floor, friend.
Girl, give good green grief.

Hard head. Heavy home hour.
Know late (last). Leave.

Let life light—little—look long.

Love matters, & maybe mind.

Morning, mother. Mother movie,
Must muster myself.

Need: new night; night; nothing;
Old own pain.

Pale past poems' purpose:
Questions.

Right room, right room.

Should somehow someone stay?
Still street, students, table.

Take tears, tell terror thing.
Think thought.

Tide, time together.
Toward tree turn voice.
Want—wild with, without words—world.

Years yet. . . .

Again, air.
Always another answer.

Away, away.

DAISY, DAISY
—my father, 1911–1984

Wrong to ask if he felt unlucky,
to want him philosophical—

he was dying—to want wisdom,
acceptance. Wasn't it his job

to show—the way—he showed
how to tie shoes, tie flies, be

stoical with tonsils and asthma
but he was indignant, insistent,

"I feel *very* lucky." Hard to watch
him struggle alone, pain on two feet;

square his shoulders, squint crazily,
his new blind eye closed. *Give me*

your answer, sang my head, *do*. Stupid
not to know what luck was,

not to see denial as a kind
of luck not to be interfered with.

He'd pick himself up, brush himself off,
and get back in the ring, his crony said

after the funeral—of the man who never hurt
a flyweight—re-hashing with relish

our sour history of a family store
that barely breathed, that wouldn't die:

He didn't know when to quit, your dad,
so hopeful, when the bike business—

rows of wheels, ingenious spokes,
shining handlebars, luscious primary colors—

was folding, kept his debts to himself
eked out payments, kept Hub Cycle going

until the bicycle boom. He was quiet,
he loved me, we didn't really talk,

I've made peace with that. I know he *was*
lucky to have seen his life through

an optimist's lens, Sundays cycling past
the disappearing meadows of wildflowers,

the new turnpike, that view his luck—
not teachable—born to a lyric world

he'd refuse to admit the underbelly of

where you'd look sweet upon the seat
of a bicycle built for two

POEM AT THE END OF AUGUST

Too late to be a cosmologist—or athletic.
Too late for the illusion of a limitless *later* . . .

Once I knew what was required of me:
Patience. Vigilance. Kindness.

And what I required of myself:
empathy *and* selfishness;

to face the discomfiting asymmetries of truth;
also, to make something from them;

and wit—
the wit to make it all work.

———

Lunch on the pier with C,
lunch I like to call Killer of the Dream.

The dream: to spend *all* of a day moving inside the poem.

But then, affection, gossip, bread,
a balloonist and gulls overhead—

the conversation of others, tantalizing
late summer confidences, familiar, naked—

yet dull—

and then, like the shock of undertow,
my own wordless vortex, engulfing,

nullifying, near this summer's end.

———

Luxe, calme, et volupté. . . .

Twilight pinks the sky along the back shore,
streaking the quiet of the bay.

Across the empty Grand Union parking lot,
two coyotes move, brazen with hunger,

scavenging the macadam.

Why are they in Provincetown,
how did they cross the Canal—

over the Sagamore bridge, at night?

At the edge of the lot, an invisible bird
babbling in a tree of sudden gold.

———

My name means "a father rejoices." My father died
in 1984, a year I'd been sure was fictional.

Manuel was my father; my son is Daniel,

my grandfathers, Isaac and Jacob.
Was I a Gail that gave a father joy?

Was that what I was, that what I was for?

———

My. My. My. My city, my harbor, my politics.
My children, my husband, my labors,

my remorse, my griefs—

this year's blue notebook, half its lines crossed out,
its margins full of question marks.

———

You must take your life in your mouth now,
Gail, the way a mother cat, sensing threat to her litter,

carries each kitten by the scruff of the neck
between her sharp teeth

to a place where it can't be harmed.

———

Luxe, calme, et volupté. . . .

Outside my window, two children on the beach,
brother and sister. The boy, running toward her,

calls *I have good news and bad!*

And the girl cries gleefully, *Tell the bad! Tell the bad!*
subversive girl, thrilling for experience—

then they're out of earshot, gone.